My Lazarus Experience

A PANDEMIC MIRACLE

Nyzia Nij'a

S.H.E. PUBLISHING, LLC

THE LAZARUS EXPERIENCE
Copyright © 2024 by Nyzia Nij"a

For information contact:

www.shepublishingllc.com | info@shepublishingllc.com

Cover and Title Page Design by Michelle Phillips of CHELLD3 3D VISUALIZATION AND DESIGN

ISBN: 978-1-964061-16-0

First Edition: August 2024

10 9 8 7 6 5 4 3 2 1

Foreword

Dear Reader,

You are about to read an exceptional book by a phenomenal young lady. The author of this book, Nyzia Easterling, truly exemplifies strength, determination, commitment, and dedication. Despite all the challenges she has faced and is still facing in life, she never quits; she perseveres, an attribute that she inherited from her mother, Vanessa Reynolds. There's a quote by Nietzsche that states, "That which does not kill us will make us stronger." Nyzia lives and breathes that quote. She is determined to not only leave a legacy of strength and determination to her children but also to all those she has had the privilege of ministering to through her ministry, "Saving Grace Ministries," and to all those who have the pleasure of knowing her. She has had a "Lazarus Experience," which has awakened her to do full-time ministry and helped her to realize the calling and anointing that God has on her and her life. This is her testimony and her truth, and as the saying goes, "the truth shall set you free." Nyzia is free as she is proof that despite your circumstances, despite illness, despite persecution, despite injustices, and despite loss, "if God is for you, then who can be against you?" I pray that as you read this book,

"My Lazarus Experience," you too will be free and realize your full potential, knowing that if you are determined, then nothing can hold you back. You can be revived. You can be renewed. You can be free in Christ Jesus. With God on your side, you are more than a conqueror through Christ Jesus.

"For I know the plans I have for you—plans to prosper you and not harm you, plans to give you hope and a future." (Jeremiah 29:11).

Written by Penny N. Rodgers, 11/15/22

Contents

The Celebration

CHAPTER 1

The mall corridors were laced with beauty. Black, gold, and white VIP glitter sparkles extended from one end to the other. The decorations were perfectly in place, and the signing chairs were positioned. The photographer was ready to capture moments of love and celebration. The red carpet was prepared to receive the new Author of the Year. The lights were perfect, the books stacked perfectly in place, and the sounds of excitement and grace set the tone for a magical moment dreamt about for years. Family, friends, and onlookers were amazed and in awe of the ambiance set before them. Now, everyone awaited the lady of the hour. Time passed, and many awaited the author who now tells a story of being "saved by grace."

Acts 15:11 (ESV): *But we believe that we will be saved through the grace of the Lord Jesus, just as they will.*

Five minutes away, who would know the struggle of the honoree? Everything was planned and ready, with all white for adornment layering her garments of success. As she slipped into her evening outfit, she noticed her inability to use her dominant hand. Though weakness set in, it was urgent that she tried her best to get dressed and proceed to the mall where everyone awaited her arrival. The more she pressed on, the more she noticed a lack of ability to use her entire dominant side. She didn't panic; she called for help. Once dressed, she couldn't even put on her shoes without assistance. She began to pray and ask God to take over her limbs and strengthen her to make it through the night.

Finally, she arrived, adorned in white with locks of curls, ready to greet her guests. Those willing and able to support her vision and accomplishments were there. Her dedicated friend Nica, ready to sign if needed due to the weakness in her hands, escorted her to her seat. Ready to finally sign her first books and share her testimony to give hope to others, she sat in place and smiled with grace.

Ephesians 4:7 (NIV): *"But to each one of us grace has been given as Christ apportioned it."*

The author of the hour now signed books and took pictures, embracing the guests with class and joy. Pressing through her numb and tingling extremities, she continued to pray and ask God to hold her up. Book after book, picture after picture, all she could do was thank God for keeping her strong enough to make it through it all. After such an amazing evening at her book signing, she, with assistance, attended her after-party at the one and only Café Lamberti's and celebrated with her family and friends. Great food, delicious desserts from the one and only Kreemies Bakery, and words of great encouragement and inspiration filled the room. No one knew of her agony but her friend Nica and God. Finally, the night had come to an end, and the return to reality set in. Tears fell, but fear never set in. "Through it all again, I made it through, and now if I could just make it through the night." Quickly falling to sleep still not knowing what was going on, she trusted God to keep her and slept like a baby.

James 1:6 (NIV): *But when you ask, you must believe and not doubt, because the one who doubts is like a wave of the sea, blown and tossed by the wind.*

Healing Notes

Question: Have you ever planned a celebration, and it didn't go quite as planned? Have you ever pursued a dream that didn't come out the way you envisioned it?

Hebrews 11:1 (NIV): *"Now faith is confidence in what we hope for and assurance about what we do not see."*

The morning came, and she arose with great faith and no fear, just concern and confidence that this too shall pass. Soon after awakening, she called the doctor and explained her symptoms. With concern, she was called in and seen. Blood work was administered, and the waiting game began. One week later, she returned for a follow-up visit and was told that her body had a reaction to the COVID shot number one. Due to her previous diagnosis of sarcoidosis and MS, she was advised by all specialists and doctors to receive the vaccine so she would not have a high risk of death. Not realizing at the time that she needed to have more faith in God than in the doctors, she took their advice. Two weeks passed, and despite the fact her feelings did not return, she proceeded with COVID shot number two. While others were vaccinated and had no reaction at all, maybe sore arms for a few days, things turned horrific for the woman who prayed and cried, asking for her strength back. In fact, now the entire opposite side lost full extremities, leaving her paralyzed. Now the feeling shifted to more misery with consistent body spasms that embraced her entire body, giving off feelings of being torched in flames before slight relief became available. The spasms increased over time to almost 52 an hour, and all she could do was cry and pray.

From Cooper Hospital to Jefferson Health repeatedly for a few months, there was little or no relief. Every doctor, specialist, and herbalist by this time had no answers. The trial guinea pig experiments began, while the entire time the pain increased, and spasms continued to torch this beautiful soul from the inside out. Due to many not knowing what the

COVID shot contained and the given symptoms having nothing to do with COVID, everyone was baffled.

2 Corinthians 5:7 (NIV): *"For we live by faith, not by sight."*

Calling in medical specialists who not only worked with both autoimmune diagnoses but were also so-called experts on COVID vaccines made this journey more frustrating and miserable. What do we do to save this young life with so much potential? One who walked with purpose and faith? What started as a celebration has now come to a brutal confinement. No one knew what was destined to happen. As long as they treated the symptoms to try to bring temporary relief, maybe they could find a cure. Has there ever been a time in your life when you were ready to celebrate a success of your own, and things went totally left? Did you blame God? Did you blame yourself? Can you imagine the mindset I had during this time? When you feel you have finally done something for yourself, not everyone around you but you. When you felt you had given birth to something you had helped create for a lifetime, and you wanted the world to hear. My Bible said to be angry but sin not!!! Every emotion then began to flood my mind. Hurt, defeat, anger, disappointment, guilt, confusion, and agony now took residence in my mind. Lord, was this not my assignment? Did I disobey you in any way? Did I not trust you by taking the COVID shots? Please, God, answer me in this pit of hell that is now swallowing me up.

This was supposed to be a celebration of life. This was the first step to my destiny. I turned my tragedy into triumph and my pain into purpose. All I wanted to do was be a vessel of hope for those around me. Now how can I encourage myself? There is no way to give hope to a dark world when now I am hopeless and stuck once again.

John 11:40 (NIV): *"Then Jesus said, "Did I not tell you that if you believe, you will see the glory of God?"*

I know you said you would never leave or forsake me, God, yet this space is painful, and I don't feel you in this place. Have you left me here? Will I even make it out? Will the real celebration be my repast as the norm that has set in to numb the people within my community? Will I be on a shirt and have a balloon release in my honor? Will my children be, okay? All these questions set in when I could no longer talk due to the consistent pain I was in.

I tried crying out to God, yet the pain was too intense at this time. All I could do was continue to recite to myself the promises of God.

Isaiah 41:10 (NIV): *So do not fear, for I am with you; do not be dismayed, for I am your God. I will strengthen you and help you; I will uphold you with my righteous right hand.*

Jeremiah 33:6 (NIV): *Nevertheless, I will bring health and healing to it; I will heal my people and will let them enjoy abundant peace and security.*

Psalms 30:2 (NIV): *LORD my God, I called to you for help, and you healed me.*

All of a sudden, a voice spoke to me: "Nyzia, I already died for you. You must have faith to come out of this and enough hope to be healed! Your healing will not take place until hope steps in. I know you are destined to do great things, and your destiny was determined before your existence here on earth. How bad do you want it?"

Jer 29:11 (NIV): *"For I know the plans I have for you," declares the Lord, "plans to prosper you and not to harm you, plans to give you hope and a future."*

So, as I continued to cry and moan in agony, I thought to myself, what must I do to be saved? I felt confined in a box, not knowing how to grow my faith to have enough hope to escape this torment. This destiny was now confined. It was like being buried alive. No one around you can hear the screams for life, just you and four walls. Day in and day out, I tried to make a deal with God. Okay, God, if you ease this pain, I'll do your will. I'll listen to your instructions when you speak to me at night. I'll realign my vision. Please help me!

James 1:3 (NIV): *"Because you know that the testing of your faith produces perseverance."*

Healing Notes

Question: Have you ever questioned God? Have you ever doubted His very being?

Mark 11:24 (NIV): *"Therefore, I tell you, whatever you ask for in prayer, believe that you have received it, and it will be yours."*

My thoughts went to the biblical story of Lazarus. When Lazarus became sick, his sisters went to Jesus and said, "Jesus, the one you love is sick!" I started to question if He really loved me. God, the daughter you love is sick. The one who loves everyone and helps everyone. The daughter who seeks you for guidance and love in every step she takes. Yes, Lord, it's me. I need you now. This doesn't make sense anymore. Why are you not responding to my cry, God? I am dying inside, and now I need you before I give up.

Guess what? In my mind, He did not come when I wanted Him to. So, I died inside first. I tried to grab hold of my destiny factors and the promises I made to myself, yet I didn't have enough hope to heal. God's love was to be trusted, and I failed to trust Him enough. So, it was I who ruined this celebration. It was I who caused this sickness, and it was I who let my faith waver. God! I am sick. Where are you? What was the thing in my life that made all of this fall apart? Why is my faith so dim? Please don't let me die. I repeated the promises and prayed for God to increase my faith. Be careful what you pray for when you're suffering, because until I learned patience, God was not going to show up to a faithless child of God. So I now wrestled with my Lazarus in a room of containment. While wrestling with my Lazarus, I never realized I had my destiny confined. The longer I took to have faith in God and believe He would bring me out, the longer it would take for my birthing season to take place. Have you ever prayed a prayer that you didn't get an answer to? Have you ever let your faith dim when you were in a suffering place in life?

James 1:3 (NIV): *"Because you know that the testing of your faith produces perseverance."*

Destiny
Confined

CHAPTER 2

I was "Saved by Grace," and my suffering was supposed to be over. I had been in a dead state, and God saved me. So why am I here again? Tell me, Lord, speak to me. Please! Days and nights passed as I tried to hear God, never turning on the TV nor the lights—just music and me. I would hear lyrics to songs that ministered to my soul, keeping me holding on for dear life. I would hum in great pain and sing when I could face the melodies within. I would sing:

"Great is thy faithfulness. Great is thy faithfulness, morning by morning, new mercies I see. All I have needed, thy hand has provided. Great is thy faithfulness, Lord unto me."

I replayed the story in my head and could hear the words, "This sickness won't end in death." So, all I could do was worship and try to see myself heal. I began to self-search to get to my destiny. No, the doctors didn't see it, nor did the specialists who came into my room daily. They just didn't believe God's report on my life, and that was okay. I had to do this on my own. I thought about the doubt of even God's disciples. Not this soldier. I didn't plant seeds, nor did God plant seeds within me for there not to be a harvest. I didn't know what I was going through or why I had to go through it, but I knew there was a plan to push me to my destiny. The doctors gave a death note and a timeline of suffering, but I knew God's report was not that.

Matt 21:22 (NIV): *"If you believe, you will receive whatever you ask for in prayer."*

It was up to my faith to beat this thing and push out of my suffering to make it to my destiny, or give up and let the enemy win. I am nor destiny-driven. Through my tears and songs of healing, I began to seek God for my destiny. God, if you will just give me some relief so I can see and hear what you want me to do in order to do thy perfect will. Not my will, but your will be done. God, I know what my passion is, but what is the divine purpose or assignment you need me to take ownership of?

"Melodies from heaven rain down on me, rain down on me." Singing with passion, staying in worship, I never knew the aides, techs, nurses, and doctors were all being blessed in the midst of my suffering, yet I am glad I was able to be used. I started to openly invite God to come into my room and set an atmosphere of praise at all times. I called out to God and prayed for the other patients, doctors, and nurses. I even ministered to those who brought food in and out of our room.

I invited God into my place of brokenness, my disappointment, my anger, my pain, and my suffering. I invited God to mold me into a vessel from my broken pieces; I became the clay for the potter, and now, in spite of it all, I embraced God's perfect will. I was unable to see or control my destiny. What did this mean? What's my destiny now? What is destiny?

Google would say: the events that will necessarily happen to a particular person or thing in the future. Believers would say: destiny believes there is a place we reach to get to the sovereign will of God. God told Jeremiah that he was ordained as a prophet before he was formed in the womb. This teaches us that God predetermines our destiny even when we are in our mother's womb.

Jeremiah 1:4-5 (NKJV): *"Then the word of the LORD came to me, saying: "Before I formed you in the womb I knew you; Before you were born I sanctified you; I ordained you a prophet to the nations."*

Divine destiny is the destiny of God in or for a man's life. Destiny describes the course of events in one's life; organized or structured by God to fulfill His will through His divine purposes.

I realized at this point; nobody could take this pain like me. No one will ever believe the torment and agony I had to endure, no matter how many words I put this into. So God, in order for me to do thy will, what must I do to be saved? They are saying I will die, yet I know this is not your report. I know I completed many goals in life, yet this is not my divine purpose. I know you don't want me to hurt, so you're allowing this to get my attention. You have my full attention now. The tears burn my face, and the spasms torch the very soul within me. They say that this is over, but what they don't know is that my God has this whole situation in his hand, and he's giving me a stronger faith, a patient spirit, and a humble heart. He is aligning me spiritually to reach my destiny!

This room would be the room of my Lazarus. Yet when I leave here, God will make sure I get up and meet the mark He has placed on my life. Not being able to use my hands, I began to use an audio Bible. The enemy came to kill! He came to steal, and he conquered my physical body, and he had come to kill my joy and destroy my faith. See, I am not religious; I am spiritual. So I had to move from religion to relationship. So if this suffering brings me closer to God, I had to be obedient in my suffering.

Psalm 63:1 (NIV): *"You, God, are my God, earnestly I seek you; I thirst for you, my whole being longs for you, in a dry and parched land where there is no water."*

Love Notes

Question: Have you ever endured pain? Have you ever let your pain overtake your life? Did it feel like your suffering would ever end?

1 Peter 5:10 (NIV): *"And the God of all grace, who called you to his eternal glory in Christ, after you have suffered a little while, will himself restore you and make you strong, firm, and steadfast".*

Dear God, I love you, and I am willing to do thy perfect will. I will worship and praise my way through. I will continue to seek answers to my prayer: What do I do to be saved? Everything that came after I began to worship and cry out in true praise said ministry. Speak Lord! "Nyzia, you will tell your story of suffering and show the world who I am. I had to prove who I was when Lazarus died by resurrecting him from his death. Just remember your being used as a testimony, showing my grace will come with suffering. They wanted to kill Lazarus after he arose. I was the one they wanted dead, yet now he became a target also. Prepare for the rejection, backbiting, disloyalty, and haters. You must have a certain kind of faith and strength in order to be a witness for deliverance. So are you ready for your destiny or spiritual destiny assigned to ministry? Then you must study to show yourself approved. This pain is not in vain. Seek ye first the kingdom of God! Get in your word! The first scripture I came upon was: Revelation 2:10 - "Do not fear what you are about to suffer. Behold, the devil is about to throw some of you into prison, that you may be tested, and for ten days you will have tribulation. Be faithful unto death, and I will give you the crown of life."

This brought confirmation that my suffering was not in vain and trust Him that he will show up. Just as the woman with the issue of blood for 12 years, this is your time to seek my face. Still in full worship and praise, I was sent to a rehab as my symptoms of spasms decreased enough to be transferred out, and all doctors and specialists worked to get on the same page. So as they continued to work together, I continued to work toward getting healed, so my destiny wasn't any longer confined to the walls of the hospital. When I was leaving, so many people thanked me for having so much faith and the willingness to share it through my pain. The impacted lives were amazing, and it gave me more courage to trust that God was bringing healing for and through me. This helped me to reflect on the fact that there is no sickness that God cannot heal. He didn't cause this; he didn't plan for this to happen. We just live in a mean world willing to hurt and harm others. Whatever reason COVID was put out here or whatever they infused in these vaccines was not God's plan. He said the healing was in the land. I couldn't blame God for my suffering, nor could I blame him for my healing time. I had to trust this process to purpose. I continued to pray and study my audible Bible to seek clarity on the ministry placed within me. Knowing I already had a ministry, was I to revamp again, shift into full ministry, and do everything with God on it? Or do I step out and start something new? Are you calling me to start my present ministry in other states, or is this the international ministry you already spoke to me about? I replayed recent prophecies spoken over my life and continued to make sense of things.

I didn't know why I was so confused, but I knew God was good, and he was gonna lead me.

I had to first be thankful for my life because so many people had died that caught COVID or gotten the shots, so it was a blessing that I still lived. I had to recall the scripture:

"In everything, give thanks; for this is God's will for you in Christ Jesus." - **1 Thessalonians 5:28 (NIV)** In this verse, Paul taught us to give thanks in all circumstances. He also said that it is God's will. Regardless of how difficult our circumstances may be, we must find reasons to thank God. We can also be thankful that all things work together for our good if we belong to Him, as stated in **Romans 8:28 (NIV)**.

I know I still had at least 20-30 spasms an hour, and the pain of not being able to stand was so severe that I cried my way through it. I had to think about the cross. I mean, God was beaten, skin ripped from his flesh, and a crown of thorns. What did I have to complain about, honestly? When I took the time to think of all he has done for me, it's a miracle, even before this situation, that I was alive. Widowed at 25 years old, grieving mother, and suffering from autoimmune diagnoses that were more complicated than most. Then the loss of my mother, my everything. Being I wasn't prepared, I could have stayed stuck and given up, but God said NO! Stand firm and see the miracles I have planned. Just trust me. He showed me so much mercy, love, grace, and compassion that not only was I thankful, I was ready to be more generous with my healing. I just started to remind myself how blessed I was in order not to think about the present pain I was in. The more I cried, the clearer God spoke to me. He didn't dry my tears; he kept my attention. He let me see that no matter what your circumstances, you can be a blessing to everyone around you. So as I continued to suffer, I also continued to be a witness for the kingdom. I shared scriptures and sang my way through the flames my body set within. Leaving all those who came into contact amazed at my profound faith in God.

It didn't take long for me to get it. If any part of my life had been a testimony, this will be. So in spite of my pain, all I could do was thank the Lord in advance for my healing.

Nothing could tell me any different. I know that my suffering was not in vain, and my God will not let me die in it.

So I began to try and stretch my fingers and move my toes. Breathe through the torching episodes and fight back. Sip from straws and push side to side until my body would respond. There was one neurologist at Cooper who looked at me one day and said, "I'll do all I can to keep you here." Dr. Thon, who still keeps me strong with the help of God today, began to research and work closely with rheumatology as well to figure out what's next. She made sure everyone was on the same page and would not budge until they were. If anything was not to her agreement, everything was a halt. Dr. Thon then ordered me to Power Back rehab, where I then became COVID-contained.

Luke 14:27 (NIV): *"And whoever does not carry their cross and follow me cannot be my disciple."*

Covid
Contained

No visitors allowed. That was the first rule when I entered the rehab facility, and soon enough, I was in my first room. If you've ever spent time in healthcare settings like nursing homes or rehab centers, you know what the care can be like. I was vaccinated, yet here I was in quarantine, feeling like I was in a maximum-security prison. Nurses and doctors were nowhere to be seen, and the aides were often rude, coming in halfway to tend to me. After I was placed in my room, I was told someone would come back to give me a Covid test and get me settled in. But no one returned until the following day.

I couldn't move on my own and was still in the chair they left me in, with the call bell blaring red. I was furious, hungry, in pain, and frustrated. The spasms kept me from snapping out on them. All I could do was rock, cry, and hum. The pain was too much to talk on the phone without crying, and without medication, all I could do was pray.

Even though I didn't have COVID, I was being treated as if I did. I tried not to be angry because I knew the protocols were government-mandated, and the virus was taking lives in droves. I couldn't be mad at the doctors; they were just following the books and doing what they were allowed to do. What I could do was call on the heavenly doctor and ask Him to bring me back from the hell I was living in. I was faithful, but I didn't trust Him enough to avoid those vaccines. One thing was for sure—the booster was not in my future plans at all.

I began to sing again when I wasn't screaming in agony:

The blood that Jesus shed for me

Way back on Calvary

The blood that gives me strength

From day to day

It will never lose its power

It reaches to the highest mountain

It flows to the lowest valley

The blood that gives me strength

From day to day

It will never lose its power

It soothes my doubts and calms my fears

And it dries all my tears

The blood that gives me strength

From day to day

It will never lose its power

That's it! I had to turn this pain into power! I had to pray, press, push, and pull! If the doctors, nurses, techs, aides, and food services didn't know God, they would know Him through me. I refused to be here forever or be helpless as a child of the King!

I bit my hands and arms until I felt them. I kicked my legs until they stretched completely straight, enduring the pain with the cross in view. I envisioned Jesus on the cross before me, and the pain dimmed. I cried out to Jesus, "I trust you!"

Then I would sing:

'Tis so sweet to trust in Jesus

Just to take Him at His Word

Just to rest upon His promise

Just to know, "Thus saith the Lord"

Jesus, Jesus, how I trust Him

How I've proved Him o'er and o'er

Jesus, Jesus, precious Jesus

Oh, for grace to trust Him more

I'm so glad I learned to trust Him

Precious Jesus, Savior, Friend

And I know that He is with me

Will be with me to the end

Jesus, Jesus, how I trust Him

How I've proved Him o'er and o'er

Jesus, Jesus, precious Jesus

Oh, for grace to trust Him more

Jesus, Jesus, how I trust Him

How I've proved Him o'er and o'er

Jesus, Jesus, precious Jesus

Oh, for grace to trust Him more

Oh, for grace to trust Him more!

The nurses' aides would gather at my door in tears because I would talk to God out loud and worship Him. Between my spasms of agony, I kept the cross before me.

On the third day, a supervising nurse came to my room and apologized for keeping me in quarantine, even though I was vaccinated. She apologized for the lack of overnight care on my first day and for not receiving my medication. I told her no apologies were needed. My suffering had a purpose, and it was suffering that my God had allowed. She informed me that I was being moved to a new room on the next floor, where there was no fear of COVID, and it was all private rooms. I waited four hours for the transport, but at last, I was in my room. Now, equipped with the mental equipment, supplies, and a working bed, my limbs were being tried through the fire. Gloves on my hands, a band on my legs and feet, and a wheelchair to get around. I was ready to bring myself back to life.

I put gospel music on my TV and sang Leandra, Kirk Franklin, Maverick City Music, Pastor Mike, and hymns 24 hours a day. I squeezed my legs with the band open and shut, practiced weights with my hands, and used weighted utensils to try and eat, dropping them most of the time, but I refused to give up. I knew God would answer my prayers, but I had to do my part. I spun the wheels on the chair and used all assistance devices until I could take the pain. With the cross still before me, I worked this body into movement.

Weeks went by as I grew stronger. Therapists came in for physical and occupational therapy, but they couldn't believe they were also receiving mental health counseling and spiritual enlightenment by the time they left, both of us in tears.

Psalm 119:71 (NIV): *"It was good for me to be afflicted so that I might learn your decrees."*

Then the day came when I could stand on my own, thanks to the grace of God! Zoom calls with specialists and visits from in-house doctors left them amazed at my push and accomplishments. Despite the tears and Zoom appointments with doctors, medications took days to arrive. I felt discouraged, but I knew my pain had an expiration date. The only time my pain decreased was during full worship. So I never watched TV or reached out to people. I stayed in the realm of praise and worship, doing therapy with trainers and therapists, even by myself. My suffering continued, yet not in vain. I prayed more than ever.

Just as Mary cried out to Jesus with her oil, no one understood my tears, screams, or the cost of my oil in my alabaster box. Where were my friends now that I was out of quarantine? Where was my family? It was just me and God! Blood, sweat, and tears! I pressed on, keeping the cross before me. I was in a dead state, not beneficial to anyone. When would my resurrection come? Not for anyone else but for me and my kids.

"Jesus, it's me, the one you love. No one is here praying or worshipping with me. No one is here to anoint me, so I need to feel your touch! These walls are closing in, and the pain is so real. I know you won't let it take me out. I feel my strength returning. Lord, I stretch my hand to Thee! You have been so good to me, no matter how much pain I am going through. You have never failed me yet, so I am not worried. I know my due season is coming. I trust you, Lord."

I studied **Isaiah 54:17 (NIV)**: *"No weapon that is formed against thee shall prosper; and every tongue that shall rise against thee in judgment thou shalt condemn. This is the heritage of the servants of the LORD, and their righteousness is of me, saith the LORD."*

I would sing:

No weapon formed against me shall prosper

It won't work

No weapon formed against me shall prosper

It won't work

God will do what He said He will do

He will stand by His word, and He will come through

God will do what He said He will do

He will stand by His word, He will come through

I won't be afraid of the arrow by day

From the hand of my enemy

I can stand my ground with the Lord on my side

For the snares they have set will not succeed!

"Lord, I've been in this place long enough; this struggle needs to be over for me." Then the Lord spoke to me and said, "You're not ready yet! Humility is the way, and patience will guide you to full ministry."

"Okay, God, I give you my heart, my mind, and my soul. Please give me the shoulders to carry my own cross as you wipe my tears. I thank you for the miracle you will release!

Use me, God!" I prayed out loud and sang from the depths of my soul. I had conversations with techs and nurses who wanted to know God. They would stop by my room for prayer, even if not assigned to me. They stood outside my door, listening to me sing, and cried with me when I cried out to God for release. When I noticed God was working, I saw it as preparation time. Seeds were being planted for His harvest.

Studying his words had become as natural to me as breathing. Often, when you're living your best life, you might get bored or fall asleep when it's time to study, but not in my COVID prison room. This experience brought me clarity, showing me the importance of continuing to sow seeds of hope, love, and salvation even in the darkest times.

Sowing seeds of hope and love amid tears of pain, whether due to personal shortcomings, fear of failure, or uncertainty about recovery, is vital because God is always present. The impact of these actions will be abundant for the kingdom. Cry those tears, yet sow the seeds of God's mercy and grace upon the broken. Those tears can soften the hardness of the ground, like the hardened souls of men or the demons they may battle, dealing with their own "Lazarus" moments. Let them see that the Lord is always with us and will never leave us nor forsake us (**Hebrews 13:5 NIV**).

So, while I stretched my limbs, I would sing: "Yes, Jesus loves me, for the Bible tells me so." Knowing that this too shall pass, I worked out with all my strength, which at first seemed like that of a five-year-old. Gradually, it grew to the strength of a child of 12. Soon, I could feed myself and sit up at the side of the bed, surprising the occupational and physical therapists when they came in. "Hello, Mrs. Easterling!" they'd say, with awe on their faces, and I'd reply, "My God is so good to me." Then I would sing:

"Then sings my soul, my Savior God to Thee How great Thou art, how great Thou art Then sings my soul, my Savior God to Thee How great Thou art, how great Thou art!"

My therapist would then say, "Amen, let's work." "There is no doubt you will fully recover. No one has been here in as much pain as you, yet you keep smiling and speaking of your comeback. You sing and pray without worrying about what others might say. Many read the Bible or hold it while suffering, but you're different. You will be okay. I believe it, and I know everyone else does too."

Psalm 34:19 (NIV): says, "*The righteous person may have many troubles, but the LORD delivers him from them all.*"

I know this will be a testimony, as my Bible tells me to speak as though it were. I am here to plant the seed for the harvest and water it until I leave this place. You will see a blossom after my time here is over. My faith inspired me to walk the hall one day, and my hope helped me to continue walking the hall. God's grace led me to join group therapy to work out and encourage others every other day. My left side grew stronger daily, but my right side took its time. Soon, visiting hours became more available. My Aunt Lorene brought a fruit basket, Roses from the Garden of Eden in my mind. My Aunt Penny and friend Charlene brought personal items and my favorite Mickey Mouse pajamas. My friend Elite came and did my hair. Then my cousin Paula brought clothes and pajamas. My dad and Aunt Bernadette brought food. I finally got to see my children, and then I knew it was only a matter of time before I would be walking without assistance.

Still pressing through the fire, I had a conversation with God. "What do you want me to do with this crushing, with this body I thought would never be resurrected? I have sowed the seeds of hope, love, and grace. Now what, God?" God responded, "Nyzia, where are your dreams for yourself?

What makes you happy? Will you trust me enough to detach from what I've been telling you to let go of? Will you trust me enough to let go and hold on to the Master you've been singing and teaching about all these years? Will you stand in your own life and live for you? I will not allow you to continue destroying yourself trying to save everyone else. This experience has prepared you for more to come. You will now face the storms of life differently. They will come, yet your response will never be the same. The struggle will come, yet you will trust me. Get ready to be a vessel of ministry in everything you do and everywhere you go. I will take over only if you let me. Will you trust me with your life? Let me know when you're ready." Yes, God.

Revelation 21:4 (NIV): *"He will wipe every tear from their eyes. There will be no more death' or mourning or crying or pain, for the old order of things has passed away."*

Even when the administration failed me, I handled it professionally. When the food came as if I were a lost dog, and when my nurse call button went unanswered for hours, prompting me to push my wheelchair to the nurses' station to demand my medication, I still handled it differently than before my suffering. When doctors stopped my treatments because they couldn't agree, I cried, yet I remained still and waited on God. I asked myself why God wasn't rescuing me. Sometimes, as a parent, you must love enough not to rescue immediately; in relationships, love requires saying goodbye. Tough love is sometimes necessary. I was experiencing a parental moment in my relationship with God. Reflecting on the story of Lazarus, I wondered why Jesus didn't heal him from afar or why he waited so long to go to him, allowing his son to die when he had the power to prevent it. Why the wait, Lord? Everyone witnessed Lazarus's death, but how many could fathom a resurrection? I had to learn to stand for my life and be responsible, taking on a task I never imagined would come so quickly.

As my strength returned, I realized I had a life outside these walls. I needed to get home to my family and back to my business to avoid disappointing my business partner. I started guiding my home from my bed. Things at home were falling apart, so I had to pull it together. Helpless, I reached out to save my car, feed my children, restore the TV, and rescue my business from the hole it had fallen into. I began to work from my bedside, taking business calls and making critical decisions.

I had to get home, so I pushed harder to finish therapy and pressured my doctors for my treatments, which they decided

I should take at Cooper. Before long, I was brought home, yet still felt lifeless. I prayed and cried, enduring treatment #1, and returned to work, suffering through trial one.

I believed God was telling me to keep moving. I remembered the promises I made to Him about finally living for myself. So, I continued with an anthology project, partnering with amazing women with incredible testimonials. I pressed my way from a walker to a cane. Then, praying, singing, and crying, I made my way to Louisiana for a book signing and women's conference. My sister and friend Nica traveled with me as my nurse, administering my treatments. Who knew that God, still working in my down season, placed us with an anointed prophetess we called Meek Meek, full of life and favor, with her own testimonies and real trials. Meek prophesied to me, unknowingly pushing me to a place where God had breathed on me. We attended a life-changing event with a surprise guest, my then-business partner. The guest apostles and preachers spoke life into many, and one in particular resonated with me. I began to follow her ministry. She spoke life into a dead seed and brought forth a rushing wind only I could see. The enemy tried to snatch her from my life many times, but my obedience to God kept us connected.

Upon returning home, as instructed, I anointed my home from the front porch to the back doors, and I did the same at my business. Know that what is anointed by God cannot be troubled by demons. My health didn't respond to treatment #1, so I moved on to treatment #2. I began to speak against anything not ordained by God. As I recovered from an allergic reaction, I cared for a disabled aunt I inherited from my mom upon her death. We all went back home as God continued to prepare me for the road ahead. All hell broke loose, and as warned, the fire came.

Life Support

Holding on for dear life, here comes the spiral of things. I knew things and people had to disconnect after confirmation with God. However, the enemy was sending those closest to me to deter me from my divine assignment. Still humble and in prayer, I had to listen to His voice. He didn't isolate me to just be a vessel to others. He sent me as a farmer where I was needed, yet now is my pruning to birth the ministry I have within. I was waiting between four walls and yes, I stayed in worship, but there will come a time when I will accept His intimacy. If He leaves me in a place of power and responsibility, it will give me an excuse not to birth what He has planted within me. My next assignment to this vineyard is going to be an elevation the weak can't handle. I need to go back into position not for fun but for game time. I need to be ready for war. The business must go, the marriage must end, the vision must be defined, the relationship must show so that the ministry can grow. It will hurt my core, so I must get my war clothes on. I'm not dead, I'm getting in position.

I know I did my best to care for and prove myself to mankind, but now it is time for me to live and live for Him. I can never live while resurrecting everyone and everything around me. If I can't balance this out, my elevation will never happen. Now I can see, even if this fall was intentional on anyone's behalf to bring about these vaccines to destroy lives, my God had allowed this to lay me down to align my ministry with what He needed it for.

Romans 8:18 (NIV): *"I consider that our present sufferings are not worth comparing with the glory that will be revealed in us."*

I went through treatments as I took my aunt to the doctors and testing, only to find out she had cancer. So it was the sick leading the sick. Yet with the strength of God, I took great care of us both. In the midst of it all, so much was taking place. I lost my car, I lost income, my business was folding, and still, I was trusting God for clarity. Praying, crying, singing, and seeking His face. My aunt's health began to decline. Sundowners set in, no sleep, no appetite, and daydreaming of those who went on before her. Me fighting through my pain watching her decline was more painful than the physical harm I could mask.

I began to help her stay in a mind of worship. Knowing she would soon die, I tried to help her understand how grand it was going to be to see Jesus. Filling her heart with excitement and praise, we would pray, read the Bible, and sing until her eyes couldn't stay open. She transitioned to hospice at home in a hospital bed. Oxygen now kept her comfortable. Still with a smile and a ding on her heart, I would sing with her. Not knowing this would be just one of the callings in my life, I comforted her with God's words and stayed in prayer when she would moan in pain.

1 Peter 1:6 (NIV): *"In all this, you greatly rejoice, though now for a little while you may have had to suffer grief in all kinds of trials."*

Okay God, I see You birthing another testimony because if I can do this, I can do much more. Nobody wants these shoes. My, my, my, what a story this is going to be. I'm sure that when I rise, no one's gonna stop me in my calling. I pruned my prayer life, I crushed my insecurities, I armored up my heart, I studied to show myself approved, I wrote my next vision, and this visionary will move in God's timing according to His perfect will, not mine.

Okay, nobody can do what God has called me to do. It's time to take out the laptop. It's time for isolation. It's time to be on my knees in intimacy. Not ministering to others, she will. It's time for me and my master to be intimate. No more fear, no more abomination. It's time to prepare to go back in order to change the world. Not to better your community to get them ready to meet their maker. It's time for the world to bow down and pray! It's time for the one they saw suffer and stand against all odds to spread the gospel and teach.

2 Chronicles 7:14 (NIV): *If my people, which are called by my name, shall humble themselves, and pray, and seek my face, and turn from their wicked ways; then will I hear from heaven, and will forgive their sin, and will heal their land.*

I have prepared you for all the rejection, prepared you for the target set on your back. I prepared you for loss so you can produce that wholeness and produce that healing, produce that ministry and release that power within you. You will birth many books.

Jeremiah 30:2 (NIV): *"Thus says the Lord, the God of*

Israel: Write in a book all the words that I have spoken to you."

You will write many songs,

Job 19:24 (ESV): *"Oh that with an iron pen and lead they were engraved in the rock forever!!"*

Songs that will linger in hearts for a lifetime. You will then bring forth the word.

Titus 1:3 (NIV): *"And at the proper time manifested in his word through the preaching with which I have been entrusted by the command of God our Savior."*

The ministry is now set clear before me. My aunt takes a turn for the worst. I could not keep her home anymore to control her pain. So I placed her in a hospice hospital called Samaritan. There was a peace upon this place that seemed to be an atmosphere where God resided. It was not a place that looked, smelled, nor gave an impression of death. It was always peaceful, and all the staff were so loving and compassionate. The clergy was sincere and always willing to worship with us. Music therapy was the hymns we missed from being brought up in the church.

Singing:

Amazing grace how sweet the sound
That saved a wretch like me
I once was lost, but now I'm found
Was blind but now I see
'Twas grace that taught my heart to fear
And grace my fears relieved
How precious did that grace appear
The hour I first believed
Through many dangers, toils, and snares
I have already come
This grace that brought me safe thus far
And grace will lead me home
When we've been here ten thousand years
Bright, shining as the sun
We've no less days to sing God's praise
Than when we first begun
Amazing grace how sweet the sound
That saved a wretch like me
I once was lost, but now I'm found
Was blind but now I see.

What a journey for the next season has come. Never questioning God this season, test and call kept me still, worry-free, and hungry for the word. Never leaving her side, many sleepless nights, I kept my Bible, my best friend, close and dear to my heart and by my side. All I did was read my word. I placed the worship music on, and when she would awaken, she would awaken singing and smiling. I had our prayer clothes, and we prayed, and she would hold her teddy bears, and I would hold my Bible.

I knew now I was prepared to minister. Not having my own church yet, when God said go back and teach them of me, I was set to align my foundation with what saith the Lord. So if that means I'll lose folks, their season ended, no sorrow, just growth. Every part of healing must come from God. I lived it, seen it, felt it, and now must tell the world of His goodness and mercy. I had to believe it in my heart before I could teach it. We don't grieve as those with no hope, for if we live according to His will, all shall live again. I beg to bring hope to the hopeless, and no better way than through the eyes and words of one who suffered more than the average woman placed here, and she lives to tell it. I thought that would be all, aligning my present vision. Quickly, God said nope.

Broaden your lenses and expand your vision. You will not only have a NJ location for healing, but you will also have international healing hubs. Those who didn't appreciate the gifting will wish they did. You will take flights for ministry more than you vacation. You must be ready; your people need you. You will be a pastor! Who? Not me! I don't want nobody's church. I didn't say church, I said a ministry. Now study because this ministry will be beyond walls. I had to zoom in because this was not a delivery, I expected to give birth to.

Then came the dreams and visions so clearly playing out. I was teaching seminars, doing workshops, preaching funerals, anointing the sick, and marrying people—all the ways you could be in ministry while I was there. It floored me, and I was so surprised I had to share with my spiritual mother. Without hesitation, she asked, "Are you ready for your assignment? This is study time, time to be so intimate with God as if your life depended on it." So now I was on life support.

Isaiah 65:24 (NIV): *"Before they call I will answer; while they are yet speaking I will hear."*

The peace in this place was unlike anything I had ever experienced. It was as if we were in a prayer garden 24 hours a day. The enemy tried to attack me through family, friends, and even my children. But peace be still. Although I thought I was dying and sad, I realized that was not my assignment. Keeping the cross before me, I understood I had to be laid down to rise again. I needed to suffer and rest, but this was meant to be temporary, not eternal—a resting place. Christ said that the dead in Christ would rise first. My resurrection was coming as a place of elevation, but only when I was ready, in His appointed time, according to His perfect will.

I studied and prayed for 28 days consistently, just me and God, intimately. Then, I organized what my first dream instructed me to do at a women's conference. Later, I realized it should have been a healing conference. I asked my spiritual mother to be the speaker. The enemy tried repeatedly to prevent her from being the one, but what God has assigned, no man can touch. Staying by my aunt's side, I planned the conference from her bedside, and my ministry team brought it to fruition. My ordination was approaching, signaling a mighty work to be birthed. As I completed my studies, my ordination became part of the conference. I knew those who believed in me would attend, and those God wanted there would be present.

Planning to leave my aunt and return the next day was one of the hardest things to do, but I found peace knowing she was in God's arms. I left her side, and as soon as I arrived at the conference, I received the call that she had passed away. She waited until I left to take flight. I asked my team to continue the mission God had assigned. I then returned to the hospital to call the family and my sister-in-law to complete the necessary arrangements. Once my aunt's body was taken away, I returned to the sanctuary where God had appointed me to be. With great honor and anointing, I was ordained as a Pastor, and my ministry, "Saving Grace Ministries," became an outreach hub for spiritual healing. I didn't grieve but mourned, feeling peace with her transition from pain to paradise. My mourning became my morning, and no one knew what God had just done.

John 15:15 (NIV): *"No longer do I call you servants, for the servant does not know what his master is doing; but I have called you friends, for all that I have heard from my Father I have made known to you."*

Though my business was gone, my ministry was taking flight. I accepted an assignment led by God, traveling, teaching His word, and spreading healing winds through my testimony and book number 1. While living out the final chapters of my next book, I didn't realize that I would gain a new heart, a new name, and newfound love—all in Christ.

Deliverance took place from Camden to Houston as I cast away unseen things. We prayed for the return of runaways, cast out the spirit of rebellion, and helped parents with needed prayers for strength. Chains that had claimed my identity were broken, and healing was still occurring in my life so that I could claim my divine assignment.

A
Defeated
Foe

Eleven years put together and eleven years fully giving of myself for my people. At this point, it seemed to be stuck in a dry place. No funding, still out of pocket, and no location; at this point, we were discarded from the city community center. Now needing a location, we searched for a safe space for the already hurting youth. My prayers became consistent for the ministry. It was ever so quiet when answers were needed and now. Parents were calling, and youth were still dying or being adjudicated. As I prayed and prayed, God took me to the word:

Ezekiel 37:7-10 NIV *7 So I prophesied as I was commanded. And as I was prophesying, there was a noise, a rattling sound, and the bones came together, bone to bone. 8 I looked, and tendons and flesh appeared on them and skin covered them, but there was no breath in them.*

9 Then he said to me, "Prophesy to the breath; prophesy, son of man, and say to it, 'This is what the Sovereign Lord says: Come, breath, from the four winds and breathe into these slain, that they may live.'" 10 So I prophesied as he commanded me, and breath entered them; they came to life and stood up on their feet—a vast army.

Oh yes! I started to speak as though they were. I began to relay the message to all the new locations coming soon. God knew where it was. I spoke to our dry places. God then said, "Start temporarily somewhere. You need to just get the youth back in action." So, I happened to go to an event that shortly thereafter became our saving space. From youth groups and healing support classes to movie nights, we were back together again. The owner was such a blessing and patient with the ministry. She had to be sent by God in this season.

We spent our year there, and then when it was time to get funding, we were excluded because we had no location. Trying not to be hopeless, I prayed even more. "Lord, breathe on this ministry. We need you, God. Is this your will, Lord? Breathe on us." We then looked within our community and called many numbers. However, God spoke to me and said, "Go back to a former inquiry. It was not the floor for you before, but your office is ready." I reached out for the number, and when I called, I was invited to view my office. I walked inside and claimed it, anointing the doors from one end to the next. God granted me the keys, and it said, "I love you," on the key chain.

I had to speak back to the voice that said I was a defeated foe! I had to speak back to dry bones that thought they took residence. So I went to get our supplies from the center with the team, and sadly, 90 percent were ruined. When I wanted to be upset, the Lord said, "No, no, this is the beginning of a thing. No, it's not the end yet; it's your beginning. You will replace all these things, and double will be your portion!"

Psalm 46:10 (NIV): *"Be still, and know that I am God. I will be exalted among the nations, I will be exalted in the earth!"*

In 30 days, God furnished it, blessed it, and aligned it with His will. He not only set a presence of God in the center of trauma and chaos, but He also sent provision. He sent collaboration partners in the same building, He sent trainings, and set our team traveling for training to be able to enhance the skills to fulfill His will.

For eleven years, I went into the schools one-on-one or as needed. No one saw the need for trauma care. I tried to get everyone to see me as a help. Yet they saw us as an intimidating factor. Now following God's perfect will, the school board finally saw us as a necessary support team willing and able to help save lives within the school system. God now lined us up to have contracted schools and great partnerships in the city. Something we prayed for all our years in action. We had to wait on God's timing, yet His timing is always the best timing.

Continued blessings on God's behalf began to pour out on us. We were featured on the news for the Brotherly Love segment and again on how we are teaching coping skills and safety due to the growth of ghost guns in our community. Our foundation was also featured before the courts as an alternative program for our adjudicated youth. Everything I prayed for has started to come to pass.

John 15:7 (NIV): *"If you remain in me and my words remain in you, ask whatever you wish, and it will be done for you."*

When others count you out, and haters talk about you, they don't know they are pushing you to your elevation. Trust God with your dreams and all your visions within. What Lazarus has died within you? God has planted seeds within us and given us purpose before we were born. So ignite those flames within you and operate in your power within. It's time to arise and walk. Don't let anything stop you from birthing what God planted inside of you. It is time to get in your birthing position. I am determined my health won't stop me, my finances won't hinder me, my family won't delay me, and my haters won't discourage me. I am ready to push. Are you? Push through your pain, push through your blood, sweat, and tears. Push through your discouragements, frustrations, failures, and the like. Embrace your resurrection as a divine assignment from God. Nothing will be easy; adversity will have its way, yet the beauty in the birthing is all that matters. If it's your new book, your new business, your new ministry, your new career, or lifestyle, just get ready!!! You are about to see miracles, signs, and wonders. Success in God will be our portion.

Proverbs 16:3 (NIV): *"Commit to the LORD whatever you do, and he will establish your plans."*

So now that I have finally reached my birthing season, my medication started to give me excess weight, and the pain came back unbearably. Not now, Lord, not when my dreams are set in motion. My book "Saved by Grace" ranks in the top 3 of national black authors in the religious categories, and the blessing in it all was attending the conference to meet my fellow contestants and more. I need you, God, to make a way and grab a hold of my feelings. The spasms moved to my head, and the pain would ring my right ear and come through my neck into my chest. The burning was a lingering dusting of pain. I had to stay focused and block out the adversary. It was time to talk with God and work on the purpose-driven life I now have created.

I went back to the MS specialist, Dr. Thone, and she then stopped the medication and put me on a 6-hour chemo infusion to shrink the granulomas. Back to aqua therapy, PT & OT, and it kept me in great spirits and better health. So what the devil meant for bad, God began to turn it!

Romans 8:28 (NIV): *"And we know that God causes all things to work together for good to those who love God, to those who are called according to His purpose."*

The Resurrection: Miracles, Signs, and Wonders

Just as in the word of God, reflecting back on the story of Lazarus, Jesus has now appeared and removed the rocks keeping me dead in a cave. He removed every obstacle keeping me bound. He called me by name and said, "Nyzia, girl, get up! Take your grave clothes off now. Take off the layers of depression, insecurities, anxiety, doubts, loneliness, abuse, disease, and the spirits of people not attached to her next journey. Close doors that people continue to walk into that are not welcome in this season."

Many times, we bear fear and say we have faith. Just as light in darkness, when you put a light in a dark room, it illuminates, and the light shines within the room. Faith and fear cannot live in the same place; darkness must go away. When and only when you have hope and faith the size of a mustard seed will you see all of the miracles, signs, and wonders God has planned for your life. You have to get up and remove your grave clothes. Then you will become a light in this dark world, giving hope to all those around you. See, when all hope is gone, God spoke life into me: "Nyzia, get up. You will accept only my report over your life! Rise and show the world the blessings of the Lord."

Healing Notes

1 Kings 19:1-18 (NIV). *What did God say to Elijah when he was hiding because of discouragement? (Verses 9 and 13).* Did you notice that God allowed Elijah to rest for a bit? But then it was time to get up and get going.

Miracles, signs, and wonders will be your portion. You were ordained to preach my word, so get up. Let your anointing spring forth! I removed my grave clothes, and a treatment was found to push the MS diagnosis into remission and place the sarcoidosis at rest. My spirit was so humble, and the cares of this world were no longer my defeat. No more depression, no more anxiety, no more frustration, no more lack thereof. God continued to make provisions in my life to show the world that He was real. I again came off my walker and cane in order to walk around. I then was given back my sight that faded with the sarcoidosis symptoms. I was even able to breathe and drop 60 milligrams of steroids daily. He provided and paid up my rent that was overdue. He provided food and clothing for my children, and He also blessed our home with a peace that was missing for some time! God did it again! He had me speak on platforms I never expected to be on and be the guest speaker on programs and women's conferences locally to get me ready for what was to come. The demand became more than great in all areas of life, where I had to say no to many things and accept invitations according to His will only.

Yes, I still attended AQUA Therapy, PT, OT, and more. Why? To continue to gain my strength and stay healthy day by day. I had to change eating habits and increase prayer life. I began to spread the word daily, even on my social media, as God gave me a word to share. He begins to go where I am daily without realizing that people all around were watching the glory of the Lord prevail. They watch what the enemy's plan for evil be turned into God's portion of increase and deliverance.

I now was going to follow-up visits with all specialists and doctors, and they were all amazed at my progression. They always questioned my faith and were very proud of my strength—not just my physical strength, yet my continued faith in God, so much so that my Jewish doctor said to me, "Your faith saves you every time. I wish more patients had the ability to trust God the way you do."

Is there some area in your life where you've been physically or mentally down in discouragement, but now God is saying, "Get up and get moving!"? If so, look in the mirror and say, "I'm going to get up and get moving!" Then do it with all your might. God said you take the first step, and He will guide you the rest of the way.

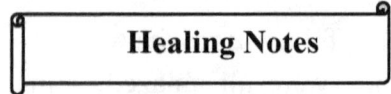

Question: What are some things you want God to grant miracles for?

I was so excited to finally begin to operate in my full calling for the Lord. Daily, the more I sought the Lord, the more humble I became. The more I could look to the Lord for every answer I needed.

It reminded me that I had to do all that God needed me to do. In this, I never knew I would begin to minister to my own family and friends. It was my 45th birthday, and I wanted to treat myself to a place I always wanted to go, so God blessed me enough to get to San Juan, PR, and it was so hot you couldn't enjoy outside in the day, so I was able to rest mentally, physically, and emotionally. Just rest.

I felt free of all responsibilities and needs of the world. The phone was not ringing every minute, and the echoes of "Mom!" didn't linger on. And for once in 2 years, the arms of a soft queen-size bed held me like a newborn baby. I was living a much-needed dream. Then, after 3 days of too-good-to-be-true excitement came the call. A call for immediate ministry for my own. FaceTime disappointment is real, so much more devastating than a voice call. With tears in her eyes, my aunt was calling to let me know that my cousin Sheema had a stroke, and she was on full life support. My heart could have stopped, yet my faith kicked in to strengthen my aunt. I said, "Go over to her and put the phone to her ear." They say your hearing is the last to go, so I encouraged her to make her calling and election sure. I prayed for healing, if it be thy will, as I also continued to stay in prayer the rest of my trip. Broken and very hurt, I continued to cover the family.

Psalm 34:18 (NIV):

"The Lord is near to the brokenhearted
And saves those who are crushed in spirit."

In my brokenness, I returned to minister to three grieving families, all the while helping my family plan my cousin's funeral. Trying to get clarity from God, I didn't know how I was going to preach my cousin's funeral and be effective in my own grief, yet God said, "I raised you for assignments like this; now you must bring a word more real than most." In conversation with God, I was given a word: "Are you ready for your appointment with God?" With the strength of God, I sang and preached a word that brought lives to God and ignited flames of hope for others. This was just one of many I knew I had to do. Therefore, I thank the Lord for all He has done in this situation and for using a vessel like me. God continued to use me in many ways.

I was releasing hope in so many ways that all you could see were blessings, miracles, signs, and wonders. I was finally operating in my calling. I then began to travel for my career of trauma healing, doing workshops and seminars, and also being a guest preacher in many places.

Tragedy hit again, and my cousin's fiancé was shot in the head. I prayed for God to grant this miracle on his behalf and save all those broken around him. So, as assigned by God, me and my armor bearer went into Penn Presbyterian Hospital with more faith than eyes could see. We set the atmosphere of glory in the ICU, then I proceeded to anoint his body. Having just gotten the bullet out of his head and part of his skull removed, he lay there looking like this may not work. But my armor bearer asked me to drop some oil actually on the head wrap on his head. Instantly, he opened his eyes and began to purge and throw up all over. His hands and feet started to move as well. Everyone in amazement, we started thanking God. His mother started raising her hands and crying, and so did my cousin. We were asked to step out of the room so they could clean him up, and so we did, still praying and thanking God for his healing in advance. We returned to the room to continue covering him. He didn't open his eyes anymore; he certainly moved his hand and foot. I continued to yet be obedient for the call and flew out to New Orleans and headed to Mississippi to a prayer summit. I went to share trauma recovery in Christ, and it was such an honor to be used in ministry. I then placed all my petitions to God in prayer. I was on the altar for many. Then I got a call from home. Oh no! I don't want to answer this call at all, but God said no to answer the phone just to hear his voice. "Cousin?" "Yes, cousin, is that you?" In all excitement, I was calling on God's name. He said, "Thank you so much, I love you! This bid is almost over." Jumping for joy! Shouting in praise, I let him know that I loved him too. Continuing to pray and thank God in advance, I came home to him being in rehab, walking again and pressing his way to gaining all strength back. Nothing more than a miracle.

God had done it again!

Psalm 51:8 (NIV)
"Make me to hear joy and gladness,
Let the bones which You have broken rejoice."

Question: Have you ever seen God's mercy in your life?
If so, write about it in detail.

Ephesians 2:4 (NIV): *"But God, being rich in mercy, because of His great love with which He loved us."*

Question: Have you ever witnessed God's mercy play out right before your eyes? What are the things you need God to turn around? Do you trust Him?

Jude 1:2 (NIV): *"May mercy and peace and love be multiplied to you."*

Continued Miracles, Signs, and Wonders!

I recalled the stories in Mark 5 when God healed the woman who had suffered from a bleeding issue for 12 years. All she wanted to do was touch Him. She crawled and worked her way through the crowd to touch the hem of His garment. Jesus asked who touched Him and said to her, "Your faith has made you whole!" It was a complete miracle of healing. In that same chapter, God healed the 12-year-old daughter of Jairus from her deathbed due to the faith of her father. He kneeled at Jesus' feet and pleaded, "Please save my child." And Jesus said, "Talitha koum!" and she arose from her bed. God has done it again!

Miracles, signs, and wonders! Notice the common number was 12. Twelve people are specially noted in Scripture as being anointed for a unique task or responsibility. The first recording of Jesus' words occurs when He is twelve years old (Luke 2:42). The New Jerusalem, which is made in heaven and brought to earth by God Himself, contains 12 gates made of pearl, each manned by an angel. Over each gate will be one of the names of Israel's twelve tribes. Christ called twelve men to bear witness to what He did and to spread the good news of the gospel to the entire world.

This year marks my 12th year in ministry. Not only has He resurrected my physical health, but He has also brought full life back to my anointing. He awakened my dreams and my desire to be used as a vessel. He awakened my faith and reassured my walk.

Oh, how great it is to trust Him. **"SHE HAS RISEN!"**

Question: What do you want to arise within you?

John 8:5 (NIV): *If thou [wert] pure and upright; surely now he would awake for thee, and make the habitation of thy righteousness prosperous.*

If you are in a period of discouragement, take hold of the faith you long for. Let's go! Move forward! Live! Learn how to dream again. Let go of anything that holds you back from a "less than" life and take hold of all that God has for you and has already placed within you. Your healing will not take place until your HOPE steps in.

Write down all the things you want to arise within you, along with your dreams and vision. You are the visionary!

Psalms 17:15 (NIV): *"As for me, I will behold thy face in righteousness: I shall be satisfied, when I awake, with thy likeness."*

Isaiah 52:1 (NIV): *"Awake, awake; put on thy strength, O Zion; put on thy beautiful garments."*

My 3 P's: Power, Purpose, and Praise

CHAPTER 7

Power (Google Definition): The ability to do something or act in a particular way, especially as a faculty or quality. For example, "the power of speech."

Power (Bible Definition): A variety of ideas relating to ability, capacity, authority, and might/strength. In human relationships, power is the authority one person holds over another.

Colossians 1:11 (NIV): *Being strengthened with all power according to his glorious might so that you may have great endurance and patience.*

Purpose (Noun): The reason for which something is done or created or for which something exists. For example, "the purpose of the meeting is to appoint a trustee."

Purpose (Verb): To have as one's intention or objective. For example, "God has allowed suffering, even purposed."

Purpose (Bible Meaning): It declares why you exist. It captures the heart of why you are on this earth and why Jesus died for you. It defines your life—not in terms of what you think but what God thinks. It anchors your life in the character and call of God.

Ecclesiastes 3:1 (NIV) *"To every [thing there is] a season, and a time to every purpose under the heaven."*

Praise (Verb): To express warm approval or admiration of. For example, "we can't praise Chris enough—he did a brilliant job."

Praise (Noun): The expression of approval or admiration for someone or something. For example, "the audience was full of praise for the whole production."

Praise (Biblical Meaning): To be thankful for God's blessings and to declare that good news to God and others.

Psalm 28:7 (NIV): *"The Lord is my strength and my shield; my heart trusts in him, and he helps me. My heart leaps for joy, and with my song, I praise him."*

I often tell my children not to allow others to take their power over their emotions because it would only result in negative actions or reactions. When you own your stuff and take your power back, no one can control you but you. It took me a long time to see that for myself. Even as an adult, there are times when you will be tested, and you must keep your power and move in grace. I always focused on ensuring the needs of everyone else were met. After this resurrection of my life, I finally realized that my life has to benefit me. I didn't know what I liked, what I enjoyed doing, or where I wanted to go. I had no fashion choice or appetite to call my favorite. I noticed that everything had died, and I had to find myself. Where does this begin? Where do I start to embrace myself and all the desires of my heart? Trying new things just never came easy for me.

My life was driven by my passion for 12 years, and my passion took residence in my heart, leaving me absent from self. I made a promise to myself that I was going to find boundaries between my passion and my purpose. My passion to help others heal and to work with broken children doing heart work and ministry couldn't end, yet I had to include myself in it all. So I again consulted the Lord and knew it was so that I wouldn't feel guilty. I would often feel guilty if I did anything for myself before others. God had to speak to me and assure me that I was doing what he required of me in ministry. He had me come into alignment with my 3 P's: Power, Purpose, and Praise.

" " Nyzia! Hear me; you have suffered for a purpose, maybe even more than many; however, you have been raised in Christ. I command you to take your POWER that you have earned. Not to exalt yourself over man yet to speak with authority and deliver healing with great compassion and conviction. You are to share your HOPE and LOVE with the world, giving the world reason to trust me. Your assignment to the ministry has shifted in order to help build the kingdom. Your very testimony will free people of bondages and doubt. You have the Power to stand strong and take authority over your ministry and align it with the word. Those who adhere to my word will be saved. Those who do not will be removed. You are to operate for your purpose. I saved you for a reason, and I know what I have allowed will save so many. Your suffering was for others. You want to meet the needs of others. It's time to shift the needs from material to salvation. Nyzia, use all of your pain for your purpose. The praise thereafter will be a divine praise, not ego or pride. You asked to be used for the kingdom. So now go and declare the good works of the Lord!"

I willingly accepted my role in ministry. I made a vow to tell the world that my God can do all things but fail. I then began to take on ministry assignments preaching, teaching, and anointing the sick. I began to pray from the pit of my soul and share his marvelous works. Even in small situations, I could hear the call of God, and I would act in it and see the mercies of God unfold before my eyes. I had the enemy try to creep in and speak to my faith when a baby I anointed and prayed for died. I begged God to save this baby, but God didn't allow it. The parents allowed his organs to save others, and I had to see that one life was sacrificed for many. Understanding God knew best, I had to continue to do his will and trust Him. I continued to LIVE. The Lord had no problem reminding me that I had to live for me. I set boundaries, I learned to say no, and I was now open to hearing the voice of the Lord. I then wrote my vision to make it plain. I decided to continue to write religious books, children's books, and devotionals. I also began a new healing group curriculum for my foundation based on the healing of God. I now visit homes, anointing the entire family, and go into the hospitals laying hands on the sick. Nothing being done in its own strength, yet all being done in the name of Jesus.

I have seen with my own eyes homes shot up and no one getting hit. I witnessed sickness flee from the bodies of those who believed. I also witnessed one shot in the head, losing part of his skull, not only arose from the coma after the bullet was removed, but he now walks and talks, soon to get the skull put back in place. Miracles only the man above can do. It was always self-rewarding to help others, yet to see lives come to Christ when you deliver his word is more than gratifying—it's divine assignment in full glory. I thank the Lord for using me. I thank Him for teaching me that in ministry, you can also live. The words of naysayers don't matter as long as the kingdom is well pleased. The Bible reads:

Ruth 2:16 (NIV): *"And let fall also [some] of the handfuls of purpose for her, and leave [them], that she may glean [them], and rebuke her not."*

The call of ministry is not for everyone. The prophet Jeremiah was called to ministry before birth (Jeremiah 1:5), and the prophet Samuel was devoted to serving the Lord before he was born by his mother (1 Samuel 1:11). This call still happens today because I found it to be true. From a child, I spoke in church, sang in church, and led out worship. I took office as a young adult in the church and saw the ministry grow. I also witnessed the decline in ministry when the church failed to allow the youth and young adults to have a part in leadership. I was born and raised up in the will of God to use my gifts and talents for the Lord. Now, 45 years later, I stand before the Lord as a willing vessel. Showing the world that what the devil means for bad, God can and will turn it. I will forever give him praise, and I thank Him for my life! I came out of this Lazarus experience with clean hands and a pure heart. My focus in ministry is so intense that the level of humbleness and patience I have obtained is a miracle by itself. I am not scared to die in Christ, just not ready to abort this heavenly assignment I am on.

Yes, I have even discovered that my fashion desires are JPratt Boutique additions, my favorite restaurant is Olive Garden, and my favorite pastime is listening to prophetic worship music and writing while in a space of worship. I love water, from the shower to the pool. I now recognize that doing what I want matters as well. This experience was not the end, yet the beginning. Christ died for me to live and not die. Even when the enemy tried to say I wasn't qualified, God showed him otherwise. He tried to say I wasn't worthy, and God showed him I was chosen. He let me know that the enemy has to get permission to oppress, but he can't possess. My anointing and power in Christ make it all work out in the favor of God.

I now, without my grave clothes, walk in my full armor of God. Whether it's a school assembly, parent workshop, youth healing group, home visit, hospital visit, grief counseling, or preaching a sermon, it is ordained by God. Everyone and every call is not my assignment. God must speak to the situation. I will be forever obedient and submissive to the Lord's perfect will for my life. I learned that I am an uncommon seed that carries legacy, a legacy that carries purpose, and a purpose that holds status with authority. I don't have to try to be anything; God has already assigned me to my territory. The blood has covered my life. Now I must bring forth the word to heal the world. I am the evidence that God is a healer, provider, waymaker, and miracle worker, and I must do His will! I must live in Power, on Purpose, with Praise on my lips forevermore. I am alive!

The dead have awakened, and I am now on assignment. Go ye and tell the world I am He who heals.

Just as when Jesus visited the tomb of Lazarus and said, "Come out!" I release the garments and go. I have released the layers of death off of me, and I now walk in my calling! He has even changed my name!

Pastor Nyzia Reynolds

I will extol the Lord at all times;
his praise will always be on my lips.
Psalm 34:1 (NIV)

I will give thanks to you, Lord, with all my heart;
I will tell of all your wonderful deeds.
Psalm 9:1 (NIV)

Nothing we do or have, is of our own:

Ephesians 2:8-9 (NLT) *"God saved you by his grace when you believed. And you can't take credit for this; it is a gift from God. Salvation is not a reward for the good things we have done, so none of us can boast about it."*

Will you arise?

Healing Notes

Question: When you become a life renewed in Christ, you become a new creature. What things would you like to change or see God make new? Will you trust Him?

2 Corinthians 5:17 (NIV): *"Therefore if anyone is in Christ, he is a new creature; the old things passed away; behold, new things have come."*

Isaiah 11:1-9 (NIV)

Then a shoot will spring from the stem of Jesse,
And a branch from his roots will bear fruit.
The Spirit of the Lord will rest on Him,
The spirit of wisdom and understanding,
The spirit of counsel and strength,
The spirit of knowledge and the fear of the Lord.
And He will delight in the fear of the Lord,
And He will not judge by what His eyes see,
Nor make a decision by what His ears hear.

NYZIA NIJ'A

ABOUT THE AUTHOR

Nyzia Nij'a (Nyzia Easterling) is a dedicated mother, sister, aunt, and friend, as well as a public speaker, teacher, counselor, grief facilitator, and CEO. Born and raised in Camden, NJ, she is the daughter of the late Vanessa O'Bryant (Reynolds) and Michael Reynolds. Nyzia is the only child of her mother and the youngest sister of her father. She graduated from Pennsauken High School, Camden County College, and Oakwood College (now Oakwood University) in Huntsville, Alabama. Nyzia is a trained Master Facilitator for trauma recovery and a specialist in Aces and deviance with the state of NJ.

Nyzia is the Founder and CEO of Saving Grace Ministries Inc., a 501(c)(3) nonprofit organization supporting families impacted by trauma, especially youth who have lost a parent or sibling to murder. Inspired by her own tragedy—the murder of her former husband in 2003—Nyzia launched Saving Grace on the anniversary of his death in 2011, with a mission to provide trauma healing, counseling, and support groups. Passionate about her community, Nyzia is committed to sharing hope with the hopeless. She enjoys singing, swimming, and loving others deeply.

Nyzia has two children, Eternity and Rashiem, and finds happiness in upholding her late husband's legacy through her work.

Message from Nyzia Nij'a: "If I can help somebody, my living is not in vain."

Available for:

- Seminars
- Healing Groups
- Grief Counseling
- Workshops
- Conferences
- Public Speaking

Contact:
Nyzia Nij'a - S.H.E. PUBLISHING, LLC (shepublishingllc.com)

FACEBOOK @savingmyhood
INSTAGRAM @savinggraceministry
TWITTER @cmdsavinggrace